Finding Beauty in Suffering

Nicola Rachel

DEDICATION

Darling Erin, this one is for you.

CONTENTS

ACKNOWLEDGMENTS

I want to start by thanking Debbie and Neil. They were both instrumental in the process of my first book. I would not be a writer today, if not for them, we truly are a tribe! Winter Swan, for the beautiful illustrations she created for this book. You've been brilliant through this process thank you, so much. To Helen, Grandad and Erin for opening my eyes to the beauty in life. Erin, a special thank you too you. I will forever be grateful that you came into my life, you showed me how to have faith in people again. My friends for understanding that I cannot always be there, because I'm either writing or struggling with my health. The patience you all have with me has not gone unnoticed. Thank you for sticking with me. To my siblings, nieces and nephews for always bringing the banter to cheer me up when things get tough. Thank you. To my parents, you consistently take interest in my writing and show me that you are proud of me every day. I am incredibly lucky. Thank you for everything you do for me. My followers on social media, thank you for the support and love, you guys' rock! Lastly, my partner and children, you guys are in the thick of it daily. Thank you for loving me unconditionally, even on days where I'm not so lovable; for getting used to me writing non-stop for long periods and stressing over editing etc. You are all incredible. I love you all.

CATERPILLAR

Toxic

Friends: we used to be good friends; forever, with a deep
connection.
It's strange when reflecting back through a looking glass
You gambled our friendship in your own personal election.

Was it fate, already pre-sealed with blood? When the hunt started
had you already picked your side? Was it easier to hide?

When the witch trials began, I didn't see you for dust; a friendship
gone all because of lust.
All because it was easier to follow your heart; you left me out in the
dark, throwing me to the sharks.

Like a hurricane exploding, taking out an entire town; you stood
back and watched as I drowned.
The words that you promised evaporated into thin air, like
discarded tissue, you threw them without any care.

Maybe it was easier for you to believe the lies, you needed someone
in your life to despise.
Foolish is the subject who believes and becomes blind; I stood
back and watched it all burn to prove fate wasn't kind.

Two final players in a game of justice, like a courtroom drama in
action all year, one of us would fall, one would cheer.
Two separate people in one messed up life, like Adam and Eve
with their apple and greed,
Yet it was you who stepped out and put us in need.

Toxicity runs through the veins of the spared, what is there left now, not one person cared.

Heavy is the crown when you're sat there alone; you battled and killed to sit on that throne.
Now we are left with the broken parts of ourselves, trying to fix them while under the spell.
Toxic is the devil and I need a saving grace, a friendship that's dead, in the past is its place.

Your Voice

Your voice can rip away my sanity
leaving my mind bleeding on the floor
Searching long and wide, for the open door
The tone so condescending upon your tongue
Ripping away at each word I speak
Your mouth makes me weak.

I block my ears and shake my head
Your voice carries echos of the past
Blood-stained tears, moments that weren't meant to last
But they did.

For too long now I've battled your voice
I've Shaken off the musical notes of your tone
If I see your name, I won't answer my phone
I'll block you out until you no longer exist
With no luck though because you only persist.

I'll become tone deaf so I cannot hear you
I'll raise my hands shoving them to my ears
No longer will your voice bring me to tears.

It's been years
No more cheers
From your voice when you've upset me
Or damaged me deeply.
No more scratching away at my head
Wishing I was dead
You're gone...

You've moved on to someone else
Your sound waves have travelled to new ears
Now she will hear your cheers
And condescending tone.

As you perch high above
On your musical throne.

It's bittersweet as she too will want to shake her head
And block her ears
Buy expensive earphones
Because it's your voice she fears.

I Want to Take Your Pain

I can't give you the one thing you crave
It's killing me.
My words are forgotten as if they have fallen from Earth
Colliding with the angels who will carry them forward.
I can ease a broken heart when love has been lost
I can help turn pain into the past and prove many relationships are
not meant to last.
I can fix someone's problems if they merely need to vent
Showing them life can be heaven sent.
I can sit and listen for hours to another's plight
Showing them the end of the tunnel is always in sight.

I can't take your pain; I can't share the magnitude of grief that races
through you with every moment they are not here.
I can't reassure you that all will be fine, for me to say this pain
won't last would be insane.
I want to bring them back to you; it doesn't leave my mind
I want to take your pain and make it all mine.
My mind is consumed with something I'll never achieve
An impossible act that is taking over me.
I fix situations, it's what I'm supposed to do
But I can't bring your favourite person back to you.
I'm angry at the world, for creating illnesses so vile;
I'm utterly disappointed with God, *for she was just a child.*
I want to fight the devil for this is all his fault.

A perfect little healer, to bring good into this world.
Life is cruel with its twists and turns, this wasn't fate.
It can't have been God's will, because he isn't filled with hate.
I wish I could take your pain; I want to change the past
So, you can create new memories, yet this time they will last.

Emotional Addiction

Your mind can be addicted to emotional pain
Get up, see a gloomy start
Your mood spirals downwards into the dark.

You're faced with opportunities, moments of hope
Your brain switches to negative, it is telling you 'Nope'.

You're working hard for the life you need
But deep in your gut you feel your emotions bleed.

Smiled at in the shop, there must be a motive
You can see it but no one else has noticed.

Angry at the world, for the choices you allowed
Wallowing in self-pity, under a dark cloud.

It's easy to believe you will keep being failed
Especially when you've had people in your life that have bailed;
From a life that's been shattered and crumbling around you
People wouldn't understand though, they haven't got a clue.

You can only blame your misfortune on the world for so long
Before it becomes the same old song.

You're now addicted to sadness, you're resentful and mad
You can't find your way back to the happiness you once had.
There should be rehab for addicts of emotional pain
Hi, I'm Nicola and I drive myself insane.

Jane

There's a story about a lady, let's call her Jane.
Jane had left school and gone completely insane.
Living a life of sin, Jane needed prayer; looking for someone to save her, for anyone to be there.

She floated through her days drifting like a cloud.
Partying her life away and making her dealer proud.
While drinking at the bar, she was dabbling with white,
To lost to see her life fly into the night.

Jane had the heart of a saint, tainted by the devil.
She was smoking green to bring her down to a normal person's level.
Kicking arse in the ring, that's where Jane did learn
To set fire to her feelings and let the suckers burn.

Over her shoulder, oh so proud; the winged man would wink.
Jane was under the ultimate spell, it happened in a brink.
Swaying over the edge, Jane was flying to close to the sun
When the winged man swooped her into his arms to show her a world of fun.

Now, Jane was blinded by his beauty and charm, for it did shine through.
Before she knew it, she was in too deep and didn't have a clue.
One fine night Jane was out having her usual good time
The winged man whispered in her ear, "Its now your time to shine".
Without a word to anyone there, Jane did up and leave
Straight in the car to do what she was good at; or so she did believe.

Pulling up to a house in an unknown location she stepped out of the car.
She went to the boot as cool as the day and picked up a metal bar.
The house was dark, stains on the walls; haunted from ghosts before
At this point in time Jane was to blind to see that she was

undoubtedly breaking the law.

A debt was owed so Jane got the girl and forced her into the home.
Her violent side rose, Janes tongue spilt in two as she got herself into
the zone.

*At sixteen years old Jane was groomed into a life of crime, she felt important,
this life was hers, it was worth every dime.*

Walking through the house the screams were so loud, but Jane was
there for a debt.
Into the kitchen with the girl, to do something she'd later regret.

After she was done, with blood on her hand's; Jane let the teen flee.
She walked out of the house and got in the car trying to remember
who she used to be.

In the bottom of the bottle Jane would check to see if her answers
were there.
She was a good person, loved her family, she was definitely someone who did care.
Shaking off the feeling and keeping herself numb, Jane carried on
with her days.
Every time the winged man called for a deed; Jane would revert back
to her same old ways.

One fateful night she was sitting at the bar when her best friend
walked in.
Out came a knife, he went straight for the winged man; angry for
causing all this sin.

In a battle against the two the knife was disarmed, Janes best friend
did leave; not before grabbing Jane, looking into her eyes and telling
her what she did need.
He begged Jane that night to get away; the winged man is up to no
good
Something in Jane wanted to listen, she needed out of this twisted
brotherhood.

Three days later Jane received a call and was told to get herself home
There was something different in her dad's voice, a very desperate
tone.

She ran down the street toward her dad, a black van parked nearby.
Jane's dad grabbed her, told her "*Don't look*" as she let out a massively
loud cry.
Her best friend was dead. Took his life; Janes world was torn apart.
Her head was spinning, eyes streaming, she couldn't feel her heart.

A promise she made on that damning night to change her ways
forever.
She shouted for God, cried out in pain, screaming "please break this
tether".

It's been many years now and Jane has kids; she turned her life
around.
Yet it shouldn't have taken that fateful night, and her best friend to
be dead in the ground; for her to realise she was under the spell of
the devil, for he had shared her bed.
She was manipulated and groomed at such a young age it fills her
heart with dread.
Her best friend lived the same life as her, but he couldn't take the
stress.
The life he was living had made him ill, he was a totally a chaotic
mess.
She remembers him every day and loves openly and loud
She now fights for the bullied, the groomed and controlled
Yet she still lives under that dark cloud.

Words Are Like Tattoos

Sticks and stones
May break your bones
But names could be fatal.

Words linger like the smell of rotten flesh
Before you know it
Who I am
Becomes who I was.

I was seven when I started getting bullied
Little insults that were merely small
She was a child after all.
They say too young to be told
So, play nice, it's the worst advice.

Seven-year-olds grow.
Their words become big.
No longer little insults
Their mouths are too big to tame
Greedy for fame.

Words broke my confidence.
Words broke my trust.
They say words can't kill you
Well, I disagree
But maybe that's just me.

Words are the foundation of the people we become.
If used carelessly
Ending lives will be done.

They are not only spoken now
But typed and sent with no remorse.
Zero accountability
We are heading off course.

Words are like tattoos.
Forever sketched into your skin
Careless little reminders of when we let our bullies in.

Ten

Ten things I wish I could ask you...

1: How can you be there, and then not be there?

My brain simply cannot catch up with my emotions.
You were here, your *heart* was beating. I heard it through your chest.

2: Why did you not explain you were depressed?

I could have helped. *Surely, I could have changed your mind?*

3: Did you ever realise you were one of a kind?

Your life had meaning you know, truly a special mind.
You were loved by so many...

4: Regrets, do you have any?

Suicide is permanent! There is no coming back from that.

5: Can I have your favourite hat?

It smells like you, and has collected fragments of your hair, the need to feel close to you is terrifying. This is the only way I know how.

13

6: Did you take a bow?

When you got to those gates, oh so pearly and white. Hmm, I hope so...

7: Why did you have to go?

There wasn't a note, *not one thing you shared.*

8: Were you scared?

At the end, while alone.
You know, I heard in support group, statistically people who die by suicide have a calmer tone.

9: Why didn't you turn off your phone?

This plays on my mind daily! If you were sure that moment, that day, was going to be the day...

10: Then why didn't you turn it off, *is it because you wanted someone to check you were ok?!*

Like you were testing fate, to give you a sign.
But no one called, so you tied the line.
You know, you broke my heart when you stopped yours!
I'm terrified now, *to open closed doors.*
I can't hear the word noose without needing to break loose.
I can't hold a tie, *without seeing you die!*
On New Year's Eve they all drink beer, for me however it's just another year.
I block the happy people out when I hear them cheer.
You didn't end your pain that night, *you merely passed it on to me*
I found a new friendship that year, their name is *PTSD*...

Fallen Angel

Fallen angel with your halo, that you use as a gun.
We used to sit within the clouds you and I, Watching the world pass us by.
Times change, so did we
Accusations thrown by you, aiming them at me
I didn't see your halo start to fall out of place, I was too busy trying to play saving grace.
The red flags were there, I didn't open my eyes
Using your halo to trip people, came at my surprise.
The colour red started to appear around your ear, yet I carried on defending you even when you weren't near.

I was summoned to the altar to answer for my sins; not one other angel was around to show that I had been pinned.
I searched for you after, I looked everywhere!
How was I to know, you'd be sitting in my chair.
You were loaded with your halo, aiming it at my head
This was the very moment; you'd make sure I was emotionally dead.

I protest my innocence, screaming for whoever could hear, my efforts were void though; you'd made sure no one was near.
The colour red now engulfed your body ready for war, your eyes glazed black as you showed me the door.
Cast out and belittled with nowhere to go; I'm hugging my halo determined that everyone should know.
I wandered around no man's land for such a long time
Stole bread, drank people's wine and committed plenty of crime.

My halo had fallen, the glow has disappeared. I had let hate and bitterness turn me into the one thing I feared.

So, I learned to be humble again, I did plenty of good deeds
I fed the people that needed it and taught the nasty a lesson on greed.
I spent my days showing people a better path to take
I got to walk through the holy land again and swam in the lake.
The glow returned to my essence, my halo back in place
Letting go of anger *was my saving grace.*

As for the cunning angel, he had fallen from the land
The tricks and the lies he had spread, had got him indefinitely banned.
It's now his turn in no man's land, yet that is where he will stay.
With his dark shaded red body, a pitchfork for a tale.
This is where he will live his days, alone, old and frail.

Glitter

She has pretty shoes, lost feet
She is bemused.
Smudged stained makeup sliding down her face
Hair swept away from a lonely place.

Cigarette burning, hanging from her fingers
The tip laced with lipstick, her mouth desert dry
Too drunk to notice, too high to cry.

Bandage on her wrist, a reminder of her struggle
Left home to soon, this beauty had her troubles.
Vacant eyes stare but no one's at home
A slave to the drugs, a nightly working clone.

The flakes of glitter fall as she stumbles to get up.
Her cherry red shoes move across the floor
Damaged eyes searching, looking for the door.

This girl yearns for her mother, she is living in silence
Leaving her family home has taken her to violence.
Staggering in the dark, she screams into the night
She's only seventeen, she is full of doubt and fright.

Within her comes a voice, courageous in tone.
Click your heals together my dear
For there's no place like home…

Men Like You

Men like you cannot change. You give decent, kindhearted and gentle men a bad name. I lived a tale of two in my life, they started with men like you.
The ones who manipulate and abuse, yet when it comes to being a gentleman, they wouldn't have a clue.

Darling this isn't my first rodeo. You mistake me for someone who is young, a girl who is coming up in this world, her journey just begun.
You're beneath me in age, you're outdated in style; for it has been bad taste to be abusive to a lady for a while.

You open your mouth and moths fly out because it's a tale as old as time. The venom you speak, the names that you shriek are not worth a dime.
You must have been taught in your life so far, that shaming a lady over her size is disgusting. Yet I can't help but wonder why you sit back with ease and believe yourself to be trusting?

Men like you, take and don't give. They groom, they mould and that's no way to live. Boys like you simply never grow in age, they merely get bigger, Louder and spit loads of rage.
It amuses me that you believe your verbal chants will affect a woman as seasoned as me. Young man, I've lived through many older versions of you; surely, you're not to blind to see? You simply don't bother me.
Were you not taught to have manners at your age? Surely, it's time you gave in and chose to fight against the rage. Seriously... at your age!

The pattern of your behaviour is predictable like a pawn on a chess board. Each tiny step you take can be deplored. Now calm your vocal cords, sit down and I'll explain. I know it's scary, but I know all about your little game.

The start is perfect. You shower with love and affection, then you go through a period of caring protection. This is a misconception, because it's not protection; it's not because you care. You simply want to remove the friends, remove the family so that not one of them is there.

Second comes shame, you make her believe she is the only one to blame! You have broken her down and shattered her soul, like a mirror falling from off a wall. While you remain ten feet tall! She has nowhere to go for comfort, not one single person who she can turn to. She has nobody else, only you!

When she finally realises and manages to flee, on your knees begging you sure will be. Remorseful and loving; a glimpse of the old you, and she will fall for it too.

The cycle will start again before she leaves for good. Now you're spiralling like an addict who is walking through the hood. You're desperate and angry, so threaten to take your life; Stabbing emotionally deeper with your verbally sharp knife.

Angry again because she did not take the bite, losing your mind because control isn't in your sight. No longer fakely suicidal, you're back and your mask has slipped. Oh, darling I believe the sociopath in you has gone and finally tripped.

The cycle starts again, but you're arguing with yourself. Nobody wants you; you've been left on the shelf. So where has this life got you? Not one person respects you. Have I hit a nerve? It's nothing that you do not deserve.

I may have gotten older; my looks may have faded. But men like you simply do not change mentally, they merely become more jaded.

Men Like You was an important poem for me. I suffered verbal and mental abuse, yet when I was going through the torture of manipulation and mind control the laws were not so strict. It's hard to prove what is verbally said. Men Like You was the catalyst for me. Writing this poem came so easy and was the final piece to the puzzle of healing from this bit of past trauma. No one has control over your mind, life, phone or mental stability. A person who wants to control what you do in life does not love you. Loving someone, is allowing them space to be themselves and not taking their identity away.

If you are a controlling person, ask yourself why? Work on that answer. Because Coercive control is illegal and immoral. If you are in a controlling relationship, ask yourself why you are? What is the worst that can happen if you leave? If you're scared, there are people who can help.

Love yourself before attempting to love anyone else. If you are in a relationship where betrayal has led you to be codependent and controlling, maybe it's time to walk away. I am huge on healthy relationships. I speak from experience when I tell you, they will still be unfaithful even if controlled. Have a healthy mindset and move on. This is for both males and females. You've got this!

Cocoon

If I Were Your Friend
My Happy Little Black Heart
Eyelashes on the Mirror
Stripped
Etched in My Mind
I Don't Text Back
Drowning
You Won't Be Broken Forever

If I Were Your Friend

I wish I was your friend at times, because I give such excellent advice, if you were to listen to me, I'd tell you to think twice. I'd sit you down and say she's not the friend you meet twice. I'd say you're losing her, like ships passing in the night. If you carry on this way you won't always be tight. It's unfortunate you know, such a heartbreaking sight, if I were your friend, I'd inform you of this plight.

She's only ever wanted what's right for you, you have no idea how much. Her emotions are a piece of art not many get to touch. She probably doesn't let anyone know it, but those emotions are soft for you, and don't tell me that I'm lying because I know you felt it too.
Maybe for a moment you felt a part of something, maybe you struggled with it more than you know, maybe it petrified you so much you had to let go.
Maybe being part of a family was too much pressure to bear, maybe you're just not used to people who care.

If I were your friend, I'd explain that not everyone wants to hurt you, in fact she's been through a fair amount of abandonment too. There may be some valid reasons. Maybe you'll always be scared, maybe being part of a family was too much, you weren't prepared. If I were your friend, I'd tell you how selfish you can be. She put you on a pedestal for all to clearly see, she was a true friend, and they are hard to come by, you had one yet did nothing at all to try.

My Happy Little Black Heart

Melt me down
Into safety pins
Give me to love.

Wear my hurt
Like war paint
Heart on my sleeve.

United we are.
One loved fused,
Together, battered and bruised.

Eyelashes On the Mirror

Eyelashes on the mirror
This girl has gone to space.
She's gone to find the aliens
To reach a better place.
The moon can offer her a shimmering light
A place to feel at home.
The stars can show her solitude
And sit her on a throne.

Eyelashes on the mirror
This boy has gone to space.
He's gone to join the aliens
He hears they're a better race.
The moon can offer him a spotlight
A place to be himself.
The stars can show him togetherness
Rather than placing him on a shelf.

Eyelashes on the mirror
Two rooms sit unoccupied.
Their parents are left weeping
For to the police, they have lied.
Asked if any troubles in the family home
Both families denied, preaching no reason was known.

Eyelashes on the mirror, their parents reminisce
Staring at the foe lashes, and all the love they missed.
The makeup and the glitter both kids were denied
Old fashioned families caught up in a bunch of lies.
Following society, not letting their children be
Whatever in the world, it is they wanted to be.

Stripped

Rip me apart you will see I bleed.
Hold my bloody heart in your palms
Watch as the beat drops.
Will this satisfy your needs?
A love lost was once mine to gain
Cut open my veins
See the undeniable pain.

Cut into my head you will see how I feel.
Place my pinkish brain into your hands
Study the map of who I am.
Does this quench your thirst?
I loved you, that was real
Dig into my memories
They were a sealed deal.

You've been given my heart
You've taken my brain
I've nothing left to give now
I've finally gone insane.
I loved you, that was real.
You murdered me, what an ordeal.

I've fixed my heart
I found this the hardest part.
Stapled it together with well wishes
It's damaged yet pumping
This will satisfy my needs.
Pouring salt on the wounds
I've sewn together my veins

No longer do I feel this deep-rooted pain.

My brain has erased memories of the past.
Bittersweet moments, not meant to last.
Washed with fluid to strip it bare
Brand new maps have formed
Ones without wear and tear.
I've a fresh journey to travel
New memories now mine to give
A new version of me ready to live.

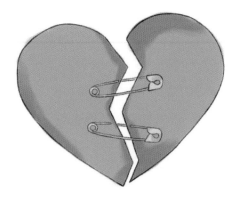

Etched in My Mind

Delusions are fragile moments they make me believe you're still here. I have you etched in my mind as clear as the daylight, I'm always holding you near and dear.

Haunted by the past and how it came to be; taking on the guilt remembering the way you last looked at me.

I guess I could pretend and make it all feel ok, but the night you walked out there were things we never got to say.

Did you know at that moment what you had planned to do? I've spent a lifetime in this traumatic limbo secretly waiting for you.

The pub and that stale smell will forever be stuck on my clothes, I won't forget the last words spoken to me, honesty you chose.

Leave and get out of the game, it's not safe for you here. I was only young; my biggest regret is that it fell on deaf ears.

The day you were found the devil stole my happiness and ripped away the sanity in me.

I begged and pleaded that it was a sick joke, this was never meant to be.

I search every day for answers you'd give and how you'd help if you were here.

Toughen up is what I'd get told, 'coz I can't always be near.

Cryptic clues in the way you spoke on those last earthly days, I didn't see it at the time, my mind was all a haze.

You've stolen my Christmas, taken New Year's Eve. they are now replaced with crippling anxiety, trauma and fear; I have nothing left to believe.

Blue is the colour of my emotions now; time is a great healer, yet I don't see how.

Missing you is hard, the night you walked out changed my life forever, now I have to wait a lifetime my friend before we can be together.

I Don't Text Back

I wake up covered in sweat, a million thoughts running through my head.
My heartbeat is pounding, so loud I swear everyone can hear it
They will wake up soon and it makes me fear it.
I sit on the bathroom floor to calm my nerves; I don't call for anyone because this is something no one else deserves.
I'm a mess.
I know it.
I own it.
But I can't control it.
These voices keep playing on repeat in the back of my head.
I get back into bed hoping for a sweet release. Lord please just grant me some peace.
It doesn't happen, sleep is non-existent, in a life that is so persistent.
On the surface I look calm, I put a front on.
Trying to prove to people that it hasn't all gone wrong... again!
But it was never right!
I live my days filled with spite,
Filled with hate, over the people that did me wrong, and over triggers that I have to certain songs.
Why on Earth am I awake at night? It's like I have these demons I fight.
They use my mind as their playground, my body as their mission
I did not allow them in, they didn't have permission.
They say you're responsible for what happens in your life, so I'm up every night trying to get this right.
Words spoken to me play on repeat
You used to be so outgoing, you used to be so neat.
Where is the person who is always there, the one we love; the one who always cares?

The girl, who will give her entire life for people to be dependent on her. You don't laugh much anymore, you're not around; you've let us down.

I'm thirty-seven years old; these words are starting to feel old.

The person you knew is no longer here.

She is saying no, but yes is all you want to hear, so let's be clear...

She's tired.

She's battered.

And emotionally drained.

All at the hands of people who have gained.

It's three a.m. (the Devil's hour)

I'm lying on the floor; my heart has gone sour.

My mind is on overload, my body rocks from side to side

I'm beaten.

I'm bruised.

Emotionally, I've died.

I don't text back straight away now; I leave people on read

All the willingness has been sucked from my soul; my battery is dead.

I swipe over apps and see messages at their plenty

I'm still a good person but my emotional toolbox is empty.

I'm flaky.

I can't live up to the person you need me to be

Apparently, I've changed, but this is the new me.

I'm no longer here to perform in your show

Something had to change, one of us had to go.

It's my turn now, and I'll start by learning how to say NO.

Drowning

Swirling around this *angry* ocean, with the waves crashing and taking
me under
I'm *lost* in a sea of thoughts; my head explodes like roaring thunder.
The cruel mistress of the tide carries me away like lost treasure to
be found
I close my eyes and drift aside, dreaming of solid ground.

No lifeboats around to save me, no whistle or glimmer of light
Left to float unconscious in my mind, drifting into the night.
The *madness* is a chaotic mess when the storms enter your *head*
Like slowly dying with no oxygen, you start to wish you were dead.

Storms pass and the ocean will tire leaving you washed up on a beach
I cough and spit the water up and see *sunshine* is in reach.
Like a washed-up shipwreck with hidden secrets, soaking in the air.
Picked up by a stranger, someone who *shows they care*.
My thoughts are now scattered and laid bare for all to see
But at least I'm no longer tormented by the thunderous ocean and
what had come to be.

You Won't Be Broken Forever

There's a version of her that didn't make it
She lay sobbing in her bed
All of the little thoughts danced through her head.

She became vacant in her mind, not one person dared to show her
an ounce of love, or that they cared.

She stopped eating, wouldn't take a shower
Her makeup used to take a while, now less than an hour.

I'd see her at times, with unkempt hair
A face so vacant, without any care.

There was something different about her
You didn't see it often, she carried pain on her shoulders
but her heart wanted to soften.

She was desperately battling some overwhelming thoughts in her
head
I heard her mutter quietly that she was probably better off dead.

I spoke with her and pleaded that she wasn't alone!
People would be there, even at the end of a phone.

Talk to me I'd say, you're worth it, your life has purpose
She cried out desperately, insisting her existence was a circus.

Let me be the clown, I whispered in her ear
I will do my best to bring you some cheer.

There was a version of her that didn't make it
She told me so, depression is very real
She had to let it go.

She had demons to fight, but couldn't face it alone
She took my advice; she picked up the phone.

The version I know now is in a much better place
I know her well; I can see the healing smile wiped across her face.

She pleaded and dragged herself through the stormiest of weather
doing what she could to break this nasty tether.

This version of herself gets up every day
She brushes her hair, and socialises
She wouldn't have it any other way.

Butterfly

You Matter
Rebel
Rainy Days
Am Writing
Empathy
Black Rose
Sunshine and Rainbows
Thanks, But no
Do Yourself a Favour
Inner Light
Captivating Darkness
I Don't Have to Say I love You
Beauty in Suffering
The Strength to Smile
It's Wonderful, This Life
Little Ways
Here's to You Dad
Stigma
Here's to You Mum
Moving On

You Matter

You matter when your arm is cut to pieces
When the sinking feeling of nothing appears

You matter when your day has been disastrous
'Coz your skin doesn't feel right in your clothes

You matter in school when the laughter starts
Because you refuse to change who you are

You matter when you do not know who you want to be
When you are being judged harshly by society

You matter when your parents do not support you
For the choices that are confusing

For every hug you need, every listening ear you require; for the
times that you feel so lost, your situation has become dire...

You matter.

Rebellious

I guess we are who we are right?
Beaten down by authority, judged by society.
We wear black clothes, "oh, there she goes, the emo, the one who cuts herself in the bath; that girl who is unhappy and can't have a laugh".
The nickname Wednesday used to be an absolute insult, according to the 'popular kids' I belonged to a cult.

Bashed and bruised for being real, outed and shamed, for refusing to kneel; to a society that wanted to fit me into their box, to zombify my brains and tie me up in locks.

They called me emo, punk, said I was a goth…

I had so many labels shoved upon my head, leaving me defenceless, wishing I was dead.
To help me through my trauma there was always music in my ears, telling me to 'fuck them'; 'coz in a few years
I'd be grateful that I didn't let them burn my soul to the ground.
It's been twenty years now and I haven't heard a sound.

Please hang in there. You've got this.

Rainy Days

Rainy days are not your favourite
Getting you out the door, has sure become a chore
Cloudy skies bring a look in your eyes
Today may be a bad one, you're longing for the sun.

You've closed off again, you hide from the rain
Afraid we'll see the bad weather and it will expose your deepest pain.
Sunny days are better for you, the rays make you smile
It's nice to see that grin so big, it has been quite a while.

Storms will come and hit like waves, it's only a matter of time
But with cups of coffee in our hands, curled up we'll be fine.
I've got a badge of honour to cope on rainy days
Secret little cheat codes I use in different ways.

I've learned to ride the waves, as they rush by up and down,
Laughing at myself, I've become my very own clown.
I know you don't like the rain; the bad weather keeps returning
You want to be you again, inside your heart is burning.

But I'll ride the storms with you, I'll even hold your hand
Until we are washed up on the beach, with blue skies and lots of
calming sand.

Am Writing

Emotions bleed from my pen, I'm satisfied
Like a sweet release of endorphins
An addiction, I'm soothed for a time.
Rainy days arrive and storm my fortress
I'm powerless to this war.
Emotions like a revolving door, am I insane?
I need something to numb this pain.
No dust, white, I don't touch a grain
So, I let the ink bleed onto the paper
It's my high. It stops the pain.
I'm a black rose in a field surrounded by colour
My beauty is cursed, it was born through trauma.
Yet I bloom, I grow like the wild ones
I flow with the wind, feel the sunshine on my face
I'm rooted; but different.
There is beauty in suffering
Just look within and see, the sooner you embrace it, the happier
you will be.

Empathy

For you to understand
Open your eyes wide
And focus on my face.
Feel the thudding of my heart
In a certain time and place.
My milky fragile features
Exhausted from the storm
With your ocean blue eyes
I can see you looking on.
Eye to eye we meet
You now feel the burn
The flames engulf your body
This is something you will learn.
You rescued me
Let me show you everlasting love
The type you only find from the heavens above.

Black Rose

Broken girls are not dead inside:
I am not pastel pink and bow tied hair
I am not sunshine on a summer's day
I am not tropical weather.
I am the destruction left behind by the hurricane
Unable to self sooth.

I do not giggle about cute outfits
Or get excited over shoes
Black is my signature colour.
I'm Doc Martens and Converse
My body displays art
My hair is very dark.
I am wild and free
Yet lost and confused
My spirit is independent
My mind tortured
I wonder through the shadows
I can't navigate my own thoughts.

I didn't invite trauma in
It was thrust upon me by evil hands
Vile mouths who manipulate.
I am not a red rose
Nor white or pink
I am a black rose, forever tainted
Through no fault of my own.

Yet here I am
Growing in the dark
Beautiful and mysterious
Damaged, but not dead inside
Not happy, yet no longer sad.

Sunshine and Rainbows

The day is warm, it's been too long
Birds are singing a medley song
The flowers are dancing, animals stare
There's calmness in the wild when no people are there.
Down in the cities where the bustling starts
In the heart of the centre the busiest parts
It's round here the stress starts to show
People rushing to and fro.
The heat is exhausting but there's work to be done
Walking along the high street is the tired mum
Stuck in the offices people want air
The barbers are sweaty sweeping the hair.
Supermarket workers are busy stacking the shelves
Teachers are learning not a minute to themselves
Care workers are giving their all to a job
The local drunk is giving the law a load of gob
The old man waves and says good morning
The postie on the morning round is caught out yawning
Sunshine and rainbows on everyone's mind
Each animal and person are one of a kind.
Calmness has settled on everyday life
With no more drama, no more strife

Thanks, But No

Barbed wire wrapped around my feet.
I'm Stumbling.
You forced me out into public
Tied in a chain of lies
Your blood-stained lips drip as the words
Fall from your mouth
I'm paralysed.
Apologies laced with poison
Stitches from old wounds break
I've been here before
I'm wiser than before!
I'm stronger than before!
So there is the door...

Thanks, but no.
No more lies
No more you and I
No more I'll change, things won't be the same.
My life is my own, it's you I've outgrown
Continue to entertain your circus
Make your monkeys dance
Keep your puppets nicely polished
Have them in a trance.

Don't invite me to your next show
I've outgrown it.
I can do without the invites
The little reminders
I do not have any care for what is new
You will always be you.
I will always be me; so thanks, but no.
Now, it's time to let me go.

Do Yourself a Favour

Do you have any advice for the younger generation?

Save yourself and fall out of love
Cupid will call on your fragile hearts many times over
Finding pure love when you're young is as predictable as finding a
four-leaf clover.
Boys don't mature as quick as girls do
It's not their fault, girls have bad habits too.
Don't expect too much from one another at such a young age
Get to know your emotions and why you feel rage.
Remember its ok to feel lonely and lost
Don't shut people out, that will later come at a cost.
If someone is nasty and tries to dirty your name
Pray for them, because clearly, they need the fame.
Be humble and respectful to those around you
When asked about the government reply with 'who'.
Dance and sing whenever you're able to
Music is the key to life; it will definitely help you.
Help others in need and don't be a sheep
You may not care now but when you are older that will
Hit deep.
Laugh. Every God given day. Laugh like a madman it will send your
doubters away.
Laughter and music are the keys to anything in life
If you can laugh at yourself, it won't hurt when others cause you
strife.
And before you settle down, make sure they are the one
Have your shit together and make sure you're the person you wanted
to become.

Inner Light

In shadows deep, where darkness lies
A tale unfolds of loves disguise.
Within the grasp of a twisted tie
A manipulative bond, I now defy.

Once entangled, naïve and blind
A web of lies, so hard to unwind.
But now I stand, with strength regained
Ready to break free, no longer restrained.

Through tears and fears, my spirit bruised
I must break free, my soul infused.
No more will I dance to your wicked tune
For in this journey, I'll find my own commune.

Like a butterfly emerging, wings unfurled
I'll soar above this toxic world.
Shackles shattered, chains released
In search of a love that's pure and peace.

No more the puppet, the puppeteer's delight
I reclaim my voice, my inner light.
I'll shed the mask you made me wear
And find my worth beyond compare.

Through valleys deep and mountains high
I'll rediscover the truth in my own sky.
With each step forward, I'll grow anew
Leaving behind the pain you put me through.

For love should lift and not confine
It should nurture souls, intertwine.
No more will I linger in deceits embrace
I choose my freedom, my hearts own space.

So here I stand, head held high
Breaking free from your web of lies.
In the pursuit of love, pure and true
I bid farewell, and I bid adieu.

To the manipulative grip, I say goodbye
With newfound strength, I'll reach the sky.
For in leaving you, I've set myself free
To embrace a future that's, mine to be.

Captivating Darkness

In the depths of night, where shadows dwell
I seek the beauty that darkness can tell.
For in obsidian realms where light is scarce
A different allure, a secret unimpaired.

Within the ebony cloak, whispers arise
Mysteries unfolding, captivating the eyes.
Silhouettes dance, their graceful sway
Painting pictures of dusk in shades of grey.

In the gloom, a canvas of endless abyss
Subtle hues emerge, unveiling bliss.
Stars like diamonds, scattered on high
Piercing the veil, adorning the sky.

Moonlight cascades, a gentle cascade
Guiding the lost, a nocturnal serenade.
Silent companions, shadows entwined
Unseen spectacles, to be keenly defined.

In this realm devoid of luminescent sheen
A different kind of beauty can be seen.
For in the dark, a tapestry unfurled
Where secrets whisper to the awakened world.

With eyes unclouded by customary light
Perceive the subtle details, dark and bright.
In the obscure, truths begin to unfold
Revealing beauty that's often untold.

So let us embrace the nocturnal sublime
Where shadows and mysteries intertwine.
For in the depths of darkness, we may find
A profound beauty that's truly one of a kind.

I Don't Have to Say I Love You

When I go shopping, I search for the sweets you like
I try to stay awake until you come to bed each night
I give you the last piece of bread, and I take the crust
I don't like football but listening to you talk is a must.
When making a salad for two, I put the bruised strawberries on mine
and leave you with the fresh ones to dine
I aim to make you laugh at least twice a day, I listen to you carefully
when you have something to say.
I run you baths when you're feeling stressed, and make you cups of
tea on days you feel depressed
When you get frustrated and find it hard to calm down, I have no
problem with playing the ultimate clown.
I forgive you on the days when you haven't been very kind, I'm
humble and patient while you find a place to shine
I support you and cheer you on when you try something new, I
respect you in private places showing loyalty is true.
I love you are three easy words to say, but showing it to someone is
better in every single way.

Beauty in Suffering

Rainy days and stormy ways are all I've known for time
There's no rainbows or sunshine in this life of mine.
Trauma came and knocked, asked me to play out
Time stood still after that, waiting for happiness to give me a shout.
Loneliness came to visit refusing to ever leave
Anger showed up in full force, I wore it on my sleeve.
I said hello to bitterness, it thought that we were mates
Sadness came by my house and took me on some dates.

Having all these lodgers was starting to take over my life
Refusing to up and leave, causing me much strife.
I found the perfect hiding place, they call it therapy
A place to sit an hour a week and finally feel like me.

Trauma was evicted, made to leave that day
Loneliness disappeared and finally ran away.
Anger left without a fight, admitting to defeat
Me and sadness had a talk and broke up later that week.

There is beauty in suffering, look within and see.
Happiness ended up shouting me, and best friends we came to be.

The Strength to Smile

You forever changed me
You will live on echoing the sweetest harmony.
Boundless and radiant, forever fluttering like a butterfly
Your beauty will flow through every ocean, every sunrise
Every sunset.
You forever changed the world.
Your laugh, your warmth, like the sun and stars
Your energy is still present and abundant.
Just like the skies at night, clear in tone.
Our dreams no you well, often you will visit them to check in.
So, every morning, every evening, I find the strength to smile
As I know you forever changed me for the better.

For Erin xx

It's Wonderful, This Life

This little life of mine
Like the rain falling down and the sunshine peeking through.
Energy ebbs and flows, highs and lows
Twists of fate, turns the tide.
Existence is a beauty and the crown of thorns awaits
I will always be a woman of wounds.
Sunlight on my face, forever overshadowed pain
Dusted down knees, springs in my feet
Like a phoenix I rise, ashes slowly fall.
Wonder and beauty, sin and regret
I rise.
This little life of mine
Not half bad.
I take the goodness, the sad, the hurt
And the pain.
A wonderful life does not come for free
I'm wild, I'm blessed yet truly; I'm free.

Little Ways

It's the little things that please me, like a walk on a rainy day
Watching the tree branches wave in the air, without a care
Feeling my boots in the dirt, a jump in a muddy puddle wouldn't
hurt.

I don't like to go out anymore, clubs and pubs are not for me
They're too loud, with a violent flow, too many lights not enough
glow.

No, I like the small things, like sitting in a coffee shop with the
people I love most. Being with my family for a lovely Sunday roast.
Reading books until my eyes are sore, writing never becomes a
bore.

I'm known for my love of mochas, especially on a cold day
I like to order my bookshelf in a particular way.
My little ways may be boring to some, but its no bother to me
I'm happy and content and there's no other way to be.

Here's to You Dad

In a world of laughter and endless delight
Where humour dances, shining ever so bright
I'll weave a poem about you dad, so dear
A man of wit, a friend forever near.

With a mischievous grin upon his face
He spins tales and jokes, leaving no trace
Of gloom or sadness in the air
For he spreads joy with his comedic flair.

His humour, like a gentle summer breeze
Tickles our souls, puts our hearts at ease
Sarcasm his weapon, wielded with grace
A master of banter, a smile on his face.

He's not just a dad, but a true friend
Through thick and thin, he'll give a hand to lend
Guiding you with wisdom, love, and care
He's always there, a rock beyond compare.

In his presence, laughter blooms and grows
A vibrant garden where happiness flows
He nurtures joy with his infectious glee
A true testament to the dad he came to be.

Through the highs and lows, he never wavers
A constant source of love, your life's saviour.
His heart, a treasure trove of stories to share
His laughter echoes, showing how much he cares.

So, here's to you dad, a beacon of light
A jester, a confidant, a shining knight
A living testament of love and fun
A dad and friend rolled into one.

May your laughter ring forever in my heart
A bond unbreakable, never to depart.
Cherish the moments, the jokes, and the smiles
For in your presence, life is always worthwhile.

Stigma

In shadows deep, where darkness dwells
A fragile soul, its tale it tells.
Within the labyrinth of the mind
A battle waged; a struggle confined.

A storm unleashed, a tempest's roar
Thoughts that haunt, forevermore.
The weight of sorrow, burdens untold
A fragile heart, left in the cold.

Invisible scars, etched deep within
Whispers of anguish, an endless din.
Fragments shattered, a fractured soul
Seeking solace, to once again feel whole.

But through the anguish, a glimmer of light
A resilient spirit, ready to fight.
With every tear shed, a seed of hope
A chance to rise, to learn to cope.

Reach out, dear one, don't bear this alone
In love and support, you'll find a home.
For mental health is not a solitary plight
Together we'll heal, ignite the inner light.

Hold on to faith, let kindness be your guide
Break the chains of stigma, let compassion reside.
For in the depths of vulnerability's embrace
We find strength and grace, our inner space.

So, let us stand together, hand in hand
Unravelling the stigma, across the land.
In this journey, we'll rise above
Embracing mental health with empathy and love.

Remember, you're never alone in this fight
Reach out, seek help, and reclaim your light.
For within your heart, a warrior resides
A testament to resilience, where hope presides.

Here's to You Mum

In a world of boundless beauty, there's a gem that shines so bright
A beacon of strength and love, guiding me day and night.
With grace that knows no bounds, and a heart that's pure and true
My dearest mum, this poem's for you.

In your embrace, I find solace, a fortress built with care
Through every storm and challenge, you're always there to share;
Your love, a gentle current, flowing deep within my soul,
Nurturing and protecting me, making me feel whole.

Like a mighty oak, you stand tall amidst the winds that blow
A symbol of resilience, a force that will never waver or bow.
You face life's trials head-on, with unwavering resolve
And in your strength, I find the courage to evolve.

Through the highs and lows we've weathered, your love remains unshaken
A light that never falters, a bond that can't be taken.
Your selflessness and kindness are gifts beyond compare
A testament to the compassion you effortlessly share.

In your eyes, I see the wisdom gained from a life well-lived
The sacrifices you've made, the lessons you did give.
You've taught me to be brave, to chase dreams without fear
To embrace life's uncertainties and persevere.

No words can truly capture the depth of my gratitude
For all the love and support, for everything you do.
But in this humble poem, I hope you feel it shine
A tribute to your spirit, an everlasting sign.

XxxX

Moving On

Bounded by choices that were not my own
A baby at the start, manipulation made me fully grown
Dragged through hell with twisted lies
Left out in the cold utterly despised.
I've shouted storms, the rain masked my tears
Left myself open, laid bare my fears.

My emotions feel like a revolving door
I hate you, but I feel the need to lift you off the floor.
We both become different versions of ourselves
With ideas in our heads, we became corrupted
Like beats of a drum, in anger we erupted.

Now, I know how low I can get
But I need to find balance
A place in my life I do not regret.
I need to find peace now, as do you I'm sure
So, lets embrace the quiet and open the door
Walk through with some dignity, white flags being waved
Now is the time. let's allow ourselves to be saved.

You can't have sunshine without the rain
You can't expect to feel hurt without any pain.
To open your eyes and see the truth, will drive you insane.
Two little puppets on strings no longer
Apart we are now, but at least we are stronger.

Moving on is hard, anger got me bad

It chewed me up and made me so utterly sad.
Spite took the driver's seat, a hundred miles an hour
Giving me palpitations, turning my heart sour.

I choose to forgive you, as you do with me
'Coz we've both reached a point of sincerity.

Winter Swan created some stunning art for this book. She is an eighteen year old art student. I am incredibly honoured she wanted some of her work featured. Thank you Winter.

Pg 5: Your Voice image.
Pg 26: Eyelashes on The Mirror image.
Pg 28: Stripped image.
Pg 37: You Matter image.
Pg 41: Empathy image.
Pg 50: Captivating Darkness image.

Reasons To Carry on

When you can't think of a reason to keep going, it's natural to feel upset or afraid. This feeling doesn't have to last forever. There are many life circumstances that can bring us to a place of hopelessness and apathy. Sometimes you might end up feeling like this for no clear reason. This is my letter to you.

Dear amazing person,

I write this with complete empathy and love, for you and life itself. Firstly, you're not alone. Although you probably do feel lonely a lot, you're never alone. Your life has absolute purpose. Perhaps you are not aware of this yet, or you are feeling so incredibly low that you do not want to accept it. Every living being has a purpose and I'm confident that you will find yours. I am not qualified, however I can speak from my own experiences. I have felt the full force of Anxiety and Depression, for me it was not being able to control my own thoughts and emotions. With time, medication and therapy I turned a corner. My Anxiety and Depression did not go, however I found away to deal with my emotions and i'm much happier for it. Everyone will be different so what works for some, will not work for others. I have felt suicidal, it was the most terrifying feeling I've ever felt. The best move I made was telling someone about it. Please do not ever be in a position where you believe you are a burden to anyone. Someone, even if it is a professional will want to help and support you.

I learned a lot about myself in the years I was mentally at my worst. In fact I had to create a new version of the old me. I found what worked for me when I felt triggered and I pushed forward everyday. Because life is precious. You never know what life has in store for you. If you're reading this and have read my previous book My Thoughts Exactly! You will see that I'm damaged; I have suffered abuse and trauma. To date, I have, Anxiety, Depression and PTSD.

Yet I still found away to see life for the beautiful creation it is. Life has an awfully ironic way of working out. Please trust that. A mixture of activities helps me daily, depending on my health (physical illnesses) I love music and cannot get through a day without listening to it. I never used to like reading, until I had my first panic attack. I found that reading calmed my nerves. At times I would read about Anxiety and the reasons it triggers, because helping myself understand it meant I was able to accept it more. Other times I read fiction because being able to step into another world in my mind was the escape I needed. I walk when I'm Anxious, because it gets my adrenaline pumping for a positive reason. There are times when I haven't been able to do any of this, so I've learnt to accept the feeling my body is choosing to receive. Telling myself it's adrenaline and it cannot hurt me. Depression was harder for to conquer; low mood is soul destroying. But I admitted defeat and let my doctors prescribe me medication. I'd rather that than feel utterly low. None of these feelings last forever.

These methods will not help everyone. But there are plenty of resources available online. I have lost two people to depression. I'm asked a lot how I cope with that. I do not have the answer. I just have to continue living. The pain I feel over that is unbearable. But I live for myself and them now.

The message I'm trying to convey here is, your life is worth it. You have things to live for. It may not feel this way right now. But you cannot predict your future. I applauded you, because living with a mental health condition can be isolating and exhausting. You have to fight harder than everyone else every day in life. I totally get it. But it also makes you a more empathetic person, and my goodness the world needs more of those. So please do continue to fight harder every day. Be gentle and kind to yourself. Every single one of you are worth this life. I invite you to write your thoughts and feelings down. Send them to me, I would love to receive them. The majority of written thoughts turn into poetry. I'm rooting for you. I love you.

All my love, Nicola xx

ABOUT THE AUTHOR

Nicola Rachel is a poet from England. She started exploring poetry two years ago while writing down her thoughts. Nicola suffers from, Anxiety, Depression and PTSD. She went on to publish two books. My Thoughts Exactly! (A collection of poetry) was published in November of 2022; her second book was a children's book for the charity Rainbow Trust, about a young girl named Erin who sadly passed away in December of 2022. The book is called Erin's Little Ladybug and was released in March 2023. Erin's Little Ladybug is Nicola's most successful book to date. It's also the book Nicola is most proud of. You can find Nicola on Facebook: Nicola Rachel- Author. Instagram: NicolaRachel.Author

Previous Books By Nicola Rachel

Available on Amazon

Printed in Great Britain
by Amazon